The Grieving Parent's Handbook

Introduction

If you are reading this, let me first say how sorry I am for your loss. I lost my son in 2008 and no one knows better than another bereaved parent how deeply the wounds of child loss pierce your heart.

While each of us grieves differently, most of us struggle with many of the same questions no matter what culture or background we were born into. It is a few of these universal questions that this handbook will address, so that when you confront them, you will have support from other bereaved parents to help you through.

All of us who have contributed to this book have lost children. The Prayer Team is a group of bereaved parents from all over the world who come together in prayer for each other's children-in-spirit. We understand the grief and sorrow that you are feeling, for we have been there. We cannot take that from you, but we can assure you that you are not alone.

Above all we extend our hands to you in friendship and support. This is a very rough road to be on, but we stand stronger when we stand together as parents helping parents.

THE GRIEVING PARENT'S HANDBOOK

CONTENTS

QUESTION NUMBER ONE

Why Me?
Pages 1-4

QUESTION NUMBER TWO

Is This MY Fault?
Pages 5-7

QUESTION NUMBER THREE

How Do I Live With This?
How Do I Move Forward?
Pages 8-12

Tips From Others
Who Have Been There
Pages 13-18

Quotes of Wisdom to Sooth
the Grieving Soul
Pages 19-22

Resources
Pages 23-24

About The Prayer Team
Page 25

QUESTION NUMBER ONE

Why Me?

"Death comes to us all; we can only choose how to face it when it comes."
— Robert Jordan

I don't know a bereaved parent who hasn't asked this question. After the loss of a child many parents feel singled out and alone. Some express feeling punished by God. You look at your friends and family members whose lives are going on just as they were, and you feel wounded, stopped in your tracks.

I think that everything is harder to bear alone. For me, what cleared up this question was my work with other bereaved parents. I came to see that I was one of thousands of parents who have and or will experience the loss of a child. When I realized that, my question changed from why me to why any of us?

Sheri Perl Migdol

I would say it's a question every parent asks after losing a child, the pain you feel is tremendous, the feeling at the moment is incredible loss. From that moment we need to hang on like when you hang on a fast ride like a roller coaster ride, since it will truly feel that way. Waves of emotion that go up and down. We need to seek help with others who have been through the most horrible thing in life, a parent losing a child. We then need to stop and try to rest and quiet our beings so that we can feel our child giving us messages from the other side that will comfort us, and let us know they're OK and still with us. We must make peace with ourselves, and know we tried our best with what we had and everything else was out of our control.

Rina Q.

The thing I've learned is ... why not me? When I got pregnant there wasn't some contract that was given to me, signed and sealed, stating that I would never lose my son. Nobody promised me that he would be with me forever. Despite the fact that I knew this from the beginning, it was still painful and it still is painful. We have to understand that just because they are infants, babies, or children does not mean that they are exempt from leaving. It is the harshest reality to ever have to face, but I think that once we learn that everyday must be lived with mindfulness and love, then the burden gets a tiny bit lighter and our actions begin to follow our thoughts. I hope this helps in some way.

Aminah J.

Knowing now how vulnerable everyone is, and how very special each life is, shaken to the core, one might want to question ... Why not me? If not me, than who?

Jean O.

Because it just happens. It just happens like the earthquakes, hurricanes, snowstorms and tornadoes.

Nancy S.

When I lost my son, "why me?" filled my mind ... over and over ... I felt detached from everyone ... felt alone ... no one around me had experienced the death of a child. A lot of their well intentioned words meant to bring me comfort angered me even more, leaving thoughts of resentment, as obviously they had not a clue how different my new normal was from theirs. One day at work I saw a post from the prayer registry ... I went to the web site and so much changed for me that day. As I scrolled the beautiful faces of children of all ages who had passed and read about these children and their families it was only then, many months after my son's passing, that I could no longer ask why me? I could no longer be angry or resentful as I scanned the pictures of all the beautiful children whose families loved them every bit as much as I loved my son.

Debbie H.

When my sister died many years ago tragically at 20 years old, my father turned against religion because he said he always prayed for his family to be safe ... that's all he wanted; and I said but if God keeps our family safe what about all the other terrible things that happen to others throughout the world. Can we truly be spiritual or religious if our own are OK but we are oblivious to the agony happening to others in the world. That's

QUESTION NUMBER ONE: WHY ME

why I never asked that question when my precious son died. As sick and devastated as I was and still am, I realized terrible things happen to people and it's not God's fault. I believe the only thing we can pray for is for God to help us cope when tragedy strikes. If everyones prayers were answered, there would be no sickness or tragedies in the world.

Lorraine C.

"Why me?" After years of contemplation, reflection, reading, and soul searching, I came to realize that I can't just ask this question when tragedy strikes. If I am going to be fair, I then must ask it when opportunity and goodness bless my existence. Life is yin and yang ... some good, some bad, some magnificent, some beyond horror, like the death of a child. Pain and blessing are part of everyone's existence. After multiple miscarriages and the death of a living son, my journey has many miles behind it; I no longer ask that question. Now I focus on how my life was blessed by their existence, however brief or long, and what lesson they taught me while I had whatever time was given to me. To remain focused on my struggles I am not free to grow. My children would want me to grow emotionally, spiritually, relationally. It's the hardest journey you will ever experience but also the most profound, if you allow yourself to feel it and reconcile with your grief.

Rose R.

"Why me?" Is a question you will search and search for an answer to but most likely never find one. Try to remember you are not alone. There are many women who have lost their baby, some never even speaking about it. Use this life changing event to bring awareness to this type of loss and keep their memory alive. God is building his army - he needs babies too!

Stacey R.

Perhaps what folks need to be asking is not "Why" but "what and how and where." I think if they can just take a step back and explore what this means - where their children have gone and what their lessons are now to learn, things might be a bit easier and really have more meaning. I found that it took less energy to explore these things than to be so immersed in grief, and it became a life lesson, as well as a healing lesson. Where are these children now and how can I connect with them? What do I need to do to make those connections and to understand about our purpose here and the contracts that we have made to learn certain lessons?

Lisa B.

You know these things happen and now it has happened to you. You thought you were doing everything right and that you had control over everything BUT, BUT!! – are you perfect? – are you God?

Susan S.

Death is random and will touch each person whether one is ready for it or not. If we can accept this, really understand this, than there will be freedom from fear. Death touches everybody, sooner or later, it'll be our turn.

Maria O.

We are all a part of something that is much bigger than our individual losses. When we come together and share our losses with each other, we get stronger. I strongly suggest that you don't hibernate, but instead seek the company of others. If you don't want to go out for a while, you can join an on-line community, (a list of resources will follow), but you need to communicate with other people who understand how you feel. You will come to see that you are not alone and that the question why me doesn't even make sense.

Sheri Perl Migdol

QUESTION NUMBER TWO

Is This MY Fault?

"To forgive is to set a prisoner free and discover that the prisoner was you."

Lewis B. Smedes

Guilt is a terrible emotion. It serves no purpose, and it can only make matters worse, however, after the loss of a child, most parents experience it. Because it has been ingrained in us that a parent is responsible for the well-being and safety of their child, when a child is lost, parents feel that they have failed. This eats away at them. What has revealed a great deal to me is my work with other bereaved parents. Through them I have been exposed to every possibly loss scenario from miscarriages to accidents, from illnesses to murders and in each case, parents found a way to blame themselves. What was clear to see from the outside was that in every case, there was nothing they could have done and that what they were asking of themselves, was to be super-human, or Godlike, with all knowledge and all power and this just isn't who we are. I began to develop mercy for myself and for all other parents when I saw how tenuous our hold really is. We may want the best for our loved ones, but we can't secure it. If we could have, we would have.

Sheri Perl Migdol

What I've learned so far is that guilt is so common after your child(ren) die. I've yet to meet a bereaved parent who hasn't/doesn't carry this feeling. Being around other bereaved parents helps each of us know that we're not alone in this, however, it doesn't go entirely away. It can at times be acute and then it ebbs. Therapy and messages through mediums are very healing. My spirituality has strengthened through my losses …"Thank you God" has gotten me through a lot of horrible times too. I guess it's a process and a lot of work. By knowing that it's "normal" and common to feel this guilt helps, otherwise the guilt gets compounded with SHAME and so many ugly emotions.

In a way, guilt on some level seems to rear its head whenever we're low physically, mentally etc. and we have to deal with it openly with ourselves ... get it out in the open and not bury it and do our best to take care and love ourselves through it.

Elsie W.

Hindsight is always 20/20 and never is that truer then when coping with the death of a child. I spent countless hours with the couldas, wouldas, shouldas, but the truth is, I didn't see those things at the time. For me, a mother's role is to protect her children and keep them safe from all harm, including death. How unrealistic an expectation I had set for myself. Some things are simply out of our control. What has given me peace is the realization that at the time I did the best I could with the knowledge and abilities that I had. They were far from perfect and probably lacking, but just as I can't change the past, I can't change who I wish I had been when I was not yet capable of that existence.

Rose R.

I just remembered what my cousin wrote to me after I lost my son. She kept it very simple and just said, "Our children are only on loan to us" ... I took that to mean that they are of the universe and that we are privileged to have them period, privileged to have them for however long they are with us. Ultimately, we are not in charge of their life paths.

Lisa B.

To answer the question over the guilt is to counter emphatically with the following questions: Are you God? Are you perfect?

Susan S.

My son was severely depressed and committed suicide 6 years ago. To this day I still wish I could have gotten him the help that he needed. I feel it was my responsibility as a parent to recognize that he was suicidal. I don't blame myself, or wallow in it, as much as I used to. In my heart I know there was nothing I could have done unless I was shown just how he felt, and if he wanted help. I feel that regardless of whether someone takes their own life, or died from an illness or some other accident, that we as parents feel it's our responsibility to keep our children safe. If one of our children passes

QUESTION NUMBER TWO: IS THIS MY FAULT

away, we therefore have failed our job as a parent. Forgiveness towards oneself in this aspect is a hard pill to swallow that takes a lot of time to digest.

ANNA P.

Guilt comes with the territory because a parent's most basic task is to protect their child. As painful and illogical as it may be, we want to know what could have prevented this. Our hearts will ache forever for what may have been ... if only.

JEAN P.

It's too hard to write about. It's too close to the pain that is unbearable for years ... Forever ... because I know in my deepest heart and soul that it was not my fault, and then in my mind, my ego, I think I could have done something to prevent her death ... Anything ... Even to the point of questioning choices I made in sixth grade or anything. It is the most desperate attempt to find a way to bring her back. Tell me it's not true and she will walk in the door alive, home from a day at school once again. So I can't think about guilt any more because it will always be there. True or not. I am her mother and I am supposed to protect her. Every cell of my body is designed to do that. Every dimension of my heart and mind is designed to do that. And it can't. So what now? Believe in who she is beyond the body and that we can forgive each other for any way we did not save each other, that we can now! With the power of the love. That goes beyond boundaries of birth and life and death. We are together in it all and it's beautiful.

KATE R.

QUESTION NUMBER THREE

How Do I Live With This? How Do I Move Forward?

"Your body is away from me, but there is a window open from my heart to yours. From this window, like the moon, I keep sending news secretly."

Rumi

If your child passes in the womb or has already lived for quite some time, the fact remains the same: your child has left the physical plane. When this happens, many wonder if there a soul. It may be something that they didn't think about before, but now, amidst the unthinkable, the question arises.

I often say that from the time you decide to become a parent, you inherit the parental mantra, "where is my child and is he or she okay?". This ongoing concern never leaves you, which is one of the reasons why losing a child is so difficult, because now you cannot answer that question. Where you used to be able to say, "the baby is right here in my womb," or "Johnny is in the backyard playing baseball," now you've got to start asking some of those universal questions like: do we have a soul, does it live on, where does it go?

I find that more people are raising questions and seeking answers than ever before because more people are outliving their children and simply needing to know!

What has helped me is this search for my son-in-spirit and finding that his essence, that which once looked out at me through his eyes, has not been extinguished. Although I could not hold on to his physical presence in my life, his soul remains close to me. I believe this connection exists for everyone and that even unborn babies are souls first, and that essence, that soul, never dies. This realization changes everything!

Sheri Perl Migdol

QUESTION NUMBER THREE: HOW DO I LIVE WITH THIS?

I discovered that in order to heal I needed to reach out to others and offer my heart. In the process I also learned my most difficult lesson, which is still a work in progress ... to forgive myself. Learning self-healing and forgiveness go hand in hand. Part of learning to love myself has involved taking care of myself. Paying attention to what I feed my body and mind, and getting outside to walk in nature or on a path, or in a park. I have discovered that for me to improve my mental health, I truly need to walk an hour a day. Being aware, listening to music (all kinds) and really hearing the passion. Offering support to others experiencing loss. It's been a little more than 2 and a half years since my son passed. Realizing this process has taken me almost 2 plus years to get to this point. I really am starting to feel good about life.

JANICE T.

I cope through advocacy. Working with people who have suffered pregnancy and or infant losses from conception through age 2 gives my daughter's death purpose.

Ironically one of my new friends is a medium who gave me the best Christmas present last year. She found me, with the most beautiful message from my daughter who wouldn't leave her alone until she relayed it. I wasn't a believer in that stuff until I forced myself to listen to her. One of the best moments in my life.

NNEKA H.

I have been helped immensely by working with a reputable medium, reading/learning about Spirit and the afterlife, and reconnecting with things that have always fed my soul (art, music, good friends, etc). The more I learn about what happens when we die (we don't) and connect to others on a similar spiritual journey, the more I am able to continue to enjoy life and continue to love and connect with my son.

AMY G.

With losing Sammi's twin, I was able to move forward as she survived. This kept my sanity these past 22 years. My heart was broken over the loss of one baby, yet I had to be strong for the other baby and that has helped me over the years. This is a loss one never forgets, but I did manage to go on.

ROSEANN H.

Losing both children and my husband I cope with therapy, prayer, keeping their memory alive, mediums and books.

NANCY M.

What helps me are my daughter's numerous love signs. Merri has shown imaginative ways to communicate with us. We thank her each time, for without her signs I would have never found joy again.

JOANN F.

The most life-impacting thing I have learned is that the way I grieve is right for me, not anyone else, and I embrace it. Whether well-meaning, intolerant or impatient, people say things. What I do is think about why and how I wake up every morning and put one foot in front of the other. It doesn't have to be done gracefully, cheerfully, or happily. It does have to be done to honor Jason and Christian. They know me, and they know how I am. Moving forward is always the goal, but I do not beat myself up if some days all I can do is breath. It takes time and practice, lots of practice, and does not happen in a short period of time. I am still learning. I have found new happiness, but I had to give myself permission to do so. Time does not heal, but love does conquer the darkness. I am and will be learning these things more every day and how to incorporate them into my life.

I had to find my own spirituality. I do get offended when people say such silly things as God needed another angel, or that the boys were not mine to keep. The first implies that God could have saved them. In my opinion that would make Him a cruel God, and I don't accept that. Besides, angels are God's creations from the beginning and the boys did not become angels because they passed, they are still my human boys! The second one just pisses me off. I have said many times, they are mine to keep and I have the scars to prove it and God does not. I have learned so much about the difference between religion and being spiritual.

My family has disappeared, but they were never fully here anyway. Their time-line for grief is probably like most others, it has a limit. When I didn't fit into their time-line, they left.

As parents, we don't want others to forget our children. I bring the boys up every day and meet the inevitable eye rolls or changing of the conversation with this: "Just because Jason and Christian aren't here physically, does not mean they aren't here in so many other ways. You talk

QUESTION NUMBER THREE: HOW DO I LIVE WITH THIS?

about your child with pride, I do the same." I know that it is my labor of love, even though sadness is always present, to never let them be forgotten. This is my honor and privilege to my last breath.

I have kept the people in my life who listen with their hearts. I have distanced myself from those who refuse to understand that I am changed, my world has changed, and the old Chris is gone. A friend said to me the other day that it has been so long, I stopped her and said, no, it was just yesterday and I am sorry that as a mother, you can't understand that. There are miles between us now. My new doctor told me that I had to put the past in the past when talking about my boys. I answered, "You have five children, which of them could you put in the past?" I did get an apology for that, thank goodness because finding a new doctor these days is hard!

I move forward each day with the boys in tow. I get through the darkest days by having some pretty heavy conversations with my boys. I cannot move through things, I have to face them head on.

CHRISTINE L.

On April 7, 2011 Zoë was hit by a car and went into a coma. Two days later she passed away from her injuries. I was given the opportunity to donate her organs. I had always been interested in organ donation, even designated it on my license at 18. This gave me a chance to have Zoë's life go on. My decision to donate helped save the lives of three little boys. Her heart was transplanted into a two year old, liver into a one year old, and her kidneys into a thirteen year old. I've had correspondence with all three families and met her kidney recipient and his family. We're all family now. I haven't experienced anything worse than the loss of my baby and now those three mothers won't have to know how it feels to lose a child. Making the choice to donate saved my life too. I've become an ambassador for my Donate Life organization. I tell people the decision to donate was a no brainier for me. If you can save a life why not?! Now there will always be someone to talk about Zoë and tell her story, so she lives on forever.

PATTI J.

I noticed that once I started meditating, I began seeing so many signs from Zac. I felt that I had to at least be accepting of what happened in order for him to be "at peace".

My family and friends changed. They blamed me and said I was pushing them away. Yet all I was trying to do was get a grasp on the fact that my son was really gone from this world.

Open your eyes and heart to the signs and they will appear.

The thing that has helped me the most is this ... if Zac was looking down at me right now, what would give him the greatest sense of peace? I didn't want him to be sad. He can't change what happened. I know he would want to see me smile again. And to find peace. I have. Oh, it still hurts. Sometimes I just have a good cry and then apologize to him and then move forward.

My best friend actually told me that because I don't believe in God, all the prayers to save my son fell on deaf ears. Is this true? Absolutely not! Even believers lose children. But the fact that my best friend said that to me ... well ... as hard as it was, I removed her from my life. I will not accept any negatively in my life any longer. I think that is a gift from my son. A gift of, in a sense, a new life. And realizing that so many things no longer matter to me.

NICOLE B.

I lost baby girl Chelsea two days after she was born. It was incredibly hard at the time. I was fortunate to have Morgan at home waiting for me. I had spent over two months in the hospital on an IV and although I was devastated to lose Chelsea, I was thrilled to get home to my little Boo Boo. I have always felt that she is my guardian angel and that she watches over all of us. I also know that she was the first person to greet Morgan when he transitioned almost 20 years later. I can't wait to meet her myself someday but until then, I try to live my life in a way that makes both Chelsea and Morgan proud. I want them to know that they are loved and remembered. I feel grateful for every day that I have been given but I no longer fear death, because I know that I will be reunited with my beautiful children.

Elizabeth B.

Tips From Others Who Have Been There

"And if I go while you're still here, know that I live on, vibrating to a different measure behind a thin veil you cannot see through. You will not see me so you must have faith. I wait the time when we can soar again, both aware of each other. Until then, live your life to its fullest, and when you need me just whisper my name in your heart … I will be there."

Unknown

They say being forewarned is being forearmed. I don't think there is any way to prepare for the loss of a child, but once you find yourself in that situation, there are some things that seem to come up for everyone. Each of us must find our own way through this maze, but by sharing what has hurt us and what has helped us, we hope to lend a hand.

Be prepared for surprises when it comes to the people in your life. I was indeed let down by some and lifted up by others. It's uncanny. One close friend of many years disappeared from my life, while another came to my side and literally camped out until I didn't need her. Some relatives said things that were deeply hurtful to me, however, one sister-in-law handed me a locket at the funeral with a photo of my son in it and to this day I treasure it. Remember that people don't know how to deal with death any better than we do, and so they can behave and speak in many unskillful ways. If you can help yourself, don't take it personally!

Sheri Perl Migdol

I have to quote Norman Vincent Peale, "You've got to SATURATE yourself with God's word." I read and read and read the Bible, I subscribed to the daily email from Griefshare (which helped tremendously); I found an outstanding grief counselor, Sharon Strauss; I clung to my friends (not many of them) who were there for me, and was in SHOCK with the many

I thought were my friends who disappeared, just vanished.

In retrospect I wouldn't worry (like I did at the time) about the insensitive things that people say: it is true, some are scared and don't know what to say; others are idiots and "know not what they do/say," and others are downright evil.

Hear it from a bereaved parent now: you are loved and cherished by God, like your darling child, you are God's and he will never forsake you. You have to hang on.

Meditate. If you don't know how, find a quiet space. Sit up. Close your eyes. Self empty. Focus on "looking". Wait for the swirly colors to emerge. If you see a white light focus on it with earnestness. Wait for it to open up into a vision for you. If you don't have success; keep trying. Keep trying. At the minimum this is serious healing at work, this quiet time, for your body to heal from the trauma.

Read PMH Atwater's books.

Get involved in a grief artwork/collage work group – strictly for grief work. You can't carry all that trauma with you all the time. You have to "get it out" of your system; attach it to paper/something/ a vessel to hold it for you.

SUSAN S.

I'll tell you the thing that helps me now. I'm alone, brother gone very young, son suicided, husband died!

I had times when my husband was out of town and I lived overseas for a while, so there were times when I was unable to see my loved ones. So now I pretend they are away in a country for which I have no visa, but one day I will, and then we'll have our joyous reunion at the "airport". Maybe silly, but it helps me.

And death ends a life, not a relationship.

SUE A.

I chose to distance myself from anyone that I felt "judged" me during my grief experience. Many friends "dropped off", and I understood. I knew it was okay. I discovered new friends. Many of the relationships developed during this period are more meaningful. I am changed. This makes sense as this had to happen for my own growth.

JANICE T.

TIPS FROM OTHERS WHO HAVE BEEN THERE

We had a reading with George Anderson ... our daughter and son-in-law came through. We clung to this communication like a lifeline, which it truly was.

JoAnn F.

I think the thing that hurt me the most was the people I worked with. My section chief and my supervisor didn't acknowledge that my son and his family had been killed. I had to call a coworker to have her ask him if it was ok if I took some time off. Then when I did go back to work I was told "It's been six months, get over it." It seemed they took advantage of my loss to get me to leave. Which I did and retired 4 1/2 years early. But I will say it was the best thing I did. Now I put all my energy into saving exotic parrots who don't have a voice either.

Donna C.

Honor whatever you are feeling. Don't let anyone "should you", you will need time to absorb, process and reconcile with your loss in the way that is best for you.
- Your grief is uniquely yours so it will look different from anyone else's, including your spouse if applicable.
- Support comes from places you might not have considered and often not where you expect it.
- Find somewhere to give of yourself and in the process, honor the memory of your child. It could be volunteering your time/skills somewhere, establishing and maintaining a memorial garden, making something positive out of something so negative by creating a foundation/educating the public/changing societal practices, etc.
- Take care of yourself: eat sensibly, exercise, get rest (even if you can't sleep), and don't accept any invitations you are not ready to.
- As hard as it is and as much as you might not want to, try to enjoy other family and friends and find opportunities to do something that you used to enjoy such as travel, music, movies. It helps to refocus for a short time and give our broken hearts a respite.
- Find an outlet where you can tell and retell your story even it is in the form of journaling. You might have to be proactive in finding a support group of others suffering child loss who truly have compassionate understanding.
- Understand that grief never ends but you will learn how to function

with it and use it to make the world a better place.
- You will never be who you used to be. People will expect you to return to who you used to be but the truth is you will have a new normal and be transformed in some way.
- Don't take comments that can be hurtful to heart, but assume people are well intentioned. Remember that before you suffered this devastation, you didn't understand the pain it shrouds you in either.
- Do things to remember your child on significant days: light a candle, set an empty place, have a moment of silence, eat their favorite meal, etc.
- When people ask you how many children you have, include them in your accounting. Because their physical presence is not here doesn't negate their relationship with you or existence (now different).
- Speaking of their relationship, continue to talk to them. They can hear you in their new dimension. It will be healing for both of you.

Rose R.

Things to do:

Just breathe

Take care of only you

Don't listen to anyone's advice

Do whatever you need to get through the day

Join a support group, if that's your thing

Find others who really do know what you are going through

Don't take anything anyone says personally - most people are clueless

Surround yourself with those who will help keep your child's memory alive

Talk about your child - those who can't handle it will leave you eventually anyway

Your time-line is your own - don't go by what others think you should be doing at any particular time

Visit your child's grave if that brings you comfort

Don't visit your child's grave if it's not something that comforts you

Don't be pressured to "move on" in any way

Don't feel obliged to get rid of your child's "stuff"

Keep whatever comforts you

Do what ever comforts you - even if for just a few minutes or seconds

Cry as much as you want

TIPS FROM OTHERS WHO HAVE BEEN THERE

Laugh as much as you can

Hold on to any happiness you encounter, even if for only a moment

Do the things your child loved to do

Eat his/her favorite foods

Connect to your child in any way that brings a smile to your face

Don't expect his/her friends to always remain close ... They will for a while but most likely will get on with their lives way before you ever do

Cry out loud. Scream if you want to

Don't do anything you don't want to do

Don't take advice from anyone!

That's my list!

Laurie M.

Looking back now through a different set of spiritual eyes, I believe the first element of moving forward was CRYING!! Just cry!!! Feel the pain and let the tears flow. I am very private so the crying was when no one could see me! I cried every day many times a day for a year. Don't fight that urge to cry!

I did not sleep but more than a couple hours a night ... so I wrote. I poured my heart on FB ... my page, Jon's page ... those hours crying and writing ... were all part of the healing ... and the responses of I got from those friends were invaluable. I had a posse of co-mourners, who were never shy to express their grief, understanding, and love. My amazing and eternally beloved husband, older son, daughter, and close friends were always within a visit or a phone call. I was a broken spirit just trying to find my way within this "new normal"... any uplifting word was comfort!

Within a month, I found a spiritual support group who believed that this life is a journey that continues beyond physical death. I needed to know where Jon was and if he was OK! I went to a healing ceremony that was facilitated by a shaman from Peru. I will never be able to say enough about that ceremony and the peace I gained from being in the presence of Jorge Delgato, which stirred my need to know more about the world unseen by human eyes.

Four months after Jon's death I met with a credible medium who validated that Jon, did in fact, still exist in the realm that I could not see. For the 1st time in 4 months, I felt a lifting of the darkness and "slight" reassurance that my beautiful boy was still alive ... unfortunately not where I could see him.

From that meeting, I began to read anything I could that dealt with life after death (credible well-known authors only) and NOTHING that talked of religious dogma ... because life after death is not bound by religious doctrine or buildings of worship. I closed many a book after reading just one judgmental line. If it didn't resonate, it was tossed. The book that opened the floodgates was *Many Lives, Many Masters* by Dr. Brian Weiss. I light went off within me and my life and beliefs about life after death have never been the same. A new thought process on life after death was deeply seated in my being. We live in a time where this information is so mainstreamed and widely accepted ... I urge anyone on this grief journey to take full advantage of this information.

I could not eat after Jon died ... I can attest to this now, but would have never told anyone back then ... I wanted to die too. Not by my own hand, but I prayed daily for death. Since GOD did not see fit to take me (as I begged morning, noon, and night) ... I had to continue on here. I lived on homemade chicken soup. A wonderful and dear friend cooked soup for months...it was all I could eat. Something in the chicken soup sustained me! I believe now it was the love that she prepared it with ... for her and her chicken soup I am forever blessed and grateful ... and I know Jon is grateful too for her saving my physical broken self.

As the weather grew warmer, I spent a great deal of time outdoors ... just talking to Jon, GOD, anyone in the unseen world who would hear ... there is something so reassuring that life goes on by really observing the outside world around us ... the sunrise (I saw many of those because I did not sleep)...the trees blooming, and dormant flowers bursting through the soil in the spring with the promise of new life.

Most of all ... the passing of time ... It becomes your best friend. At first time appears to be the enemy because time moves us away from our precious children ... but it also lessens the intensity of the pain of their crossing before us. No, nothing brings them back ... life is not the same ... life becomes separated into 2 categories "Before Them and After Them."

It is a conscious choice this grief journey and how we allow it mold us ... bitter or better. As time goes on, it is well worth it to reach out to someone else in need. This helps to take the focus off of our own grief ... if only for a short time. For our beloved deceased children, our surviving families, friends and loved ones ... we must continue on this journey and take our precious children with us in our hearts ... so when people see us ... they see our beautiful children within us! The love we have for our children never dies! This powerful love burns as brightly as the sun and its light will never be extinguished!

SONJA C.

Quotes of Wisdom to Sooth the Grieving Soul

"Death has nothing to do with going away.
The sun sets, the moon sets. But they are not gone."
Rumi

What I love about this quote is that it serves as a reminder that just because you cannot see something, does not mean that it is not there. We cannot see the sun or the moon after they have set, but we take it on faith that they are still with us. In the same way, in order to heal after the loss of children, we need to take it on faith that they are still with us in spirit. They may have been taken from our sight, but they have not been taken out of our hearts, nor has their spirit been removed from ours.

"No, no, the moments which united us are greater than centuries, and the light that illuminated our spirits is stronger than the dark; and if the tempest separates us on this rough ocean, the waves will unite us on the calm shore; and if this life kills us, death will unite us."
Khalil Gibran

What if you knew that "good-bye" only meant "so long for a time?" Wouldn't you breathe easier?

I believe that because our children are leading the way by crossing over before us, it is imperative for our sense of well-being, that we learn everything that we can about the afterlife. I have been investigating the afterlife since 1971 and for me, Danny's death was definitely not good-bye, not even so long, because we are still in touch now, only differently. This is possible for each of us.

> *"Heaven makes us human. We forget it at our peril. Without knowledge of the larger geography of where we came from and where we are going again when our physical bodies die, we are lost. That golden thread is the connection to above that makes life here below not just tolerable but joyful. We are lost without it."*
>
> — EBEN ALEXANDER, MD

I've always wondered why so many people go through life without really questioning where we came from and where we are going. Many say that until they lost a child, they had little or no interest in the non-physical realms. I believe that, in general, people are more frightened by the unknown than curious about it and therefore try to ignore it, rather than delve into an investigation of it. I believe this is a grave mistake.

The more that I learn about life in spirit, the less afraid I am. I believe that Dr. Alexander is indeed correct when he says that life becomes more joyful when we understand that we are all in-part spirit, and connected to the invisible realms of spirit.

> *"Father, tell mother she has her son with her all day on Christmas Day. There will be thousands of us back in the homes on that day, but the horrid part is that so many of the fellows don't get welcomed. Please keep a place for me. I must go now. Bless you again, father."*
>
> — RAYMOND LODGE

This quote is from a book written by Sir Oliver Lodge, who lost his son Raymond on the battlefield during the First World War. Lodge who was a scientist, was working on developing the wireless radio when Raymond passed. He and his family immediately began to explore connection with Raymond through various British mediums and this convinced the Lodge family of Raymond's continued existence in spirit.

I especially love this message that Raymond imparts to his father because it expresses something that I feel is very important, and that is this: Our children want to be remembered, talked about, laughed about and toasted to. According to my son Danny, the thoughts, love and prayers that we focus on them are gifts of energy that lift and carry them forward. The last thing any of them want is to be overlooked.

This holiday season, keep in mind that although you cannot see your child with your physical eyes, that he or she is close in spirit and just as they loved being part of the holiday festivities when they here, they want to be part of them now! Whatever holiday you celebrate, let your child's spirit be a theme that runs throughout, a theme that says: Death is a myth, eternity is real, and love is a bond that is never severed!

"Grief is not a disorder, a disease or sign of weakness. It is an emotional, physical and spiritual necessity, and the price you pay for love. The only cure for grief is to grieve."

RABBI EARL GROLLMAN

Grief is definitely not a disorder and all of us who have lost children know that to be true. It is the price we pay for the deep love we have for our children. I do not believe, however, that the only cure for grief is to grieve. Yes, we need to grieve, but grieving alone is not enough. In my opinion we need to connect-up-in-spirit to our loved ones-in-spirit and make them a part of our lives now.

I believe that each of us can cultivate a new kind of relationship with our children, one that is not based on seeing and holding them, but based on the love between us and them and on modes of communication that are indeed possible. Since my son Danny passed in 2008, I have had many "conversations" with him through numerous different means. There is no doubt in my mind that what you lose in the flesh you can find in the spirit and when you do, much of your sorrow and loneliness is lessened. In fact, it's the only real solace I know.

---

*"Life is eternal, and love is immortal,
and death is only a horizon;
and a horizon is nothing save the limit of our sight."*

Rossiter Worthington Raymond

The horizon appears to the eye to be the end, the stopping point where you can go no further. In actuality, however, we know that there is more beyond the horizon, even though we cannot see it.

The same is true for human beings, for each is endowed with a soul that cannot be seen and yet exists. When we love someone who has passed, we cannot see them but we can feel their love and their spiritual presence in our lives, if we open up to it. Now it is up to us to expand our perspectives beyond the physical horizon to embrace a universe large enough to contain both what we can see and what we cannot.

RESOURCES

SUPPORT GROUPS

Helping Parents Heal
http://www.helpingparentsheal.org
Manhattan Chapter
Chapter Phone Line (212) 283-4423
Upper West Side

The Compassionate Friends
www.compassionatefriends.org
Manhattan Chapter
Chapter#: 1158
Chapter Phone Line (212) 217-9647
Fifth Avenue Presbyterian Church
7 W 55th St
New York, NY 10019-4902
(888) 638-4312

The Forever Family Foundation
www.foreverfamilyfoundation.org
Oceanside, New York (631) 485-7523

Pregnancy Loss Support Program
National Council of Jewish Women
New York Section
241 W. 72nd Street
New York, NY 10023
212-687-5030, x464
646-884-9464

ON-LINE SUPPORT

The Prayer Registry
www.sheriperl.com/the-prayer-registry
Each child registered receives prayer annually on his or her passing date - free service - Join The Prayer Team in praying for the children.
(212) 283-4423

Open To Hope
www.opentohope.com
Grief blog with wonderful articles

Portraits By Dana
www.portraitsbydana.com
beautiful pencil sketches
Including those from an ultrasound

The MISS Foundation
www.missfoundation.org/support/achildhasdied
Providing one-to-one mentors

Channeling Erik
www.channelingerik.com
Erik, who passed in 2008, provides information to his readers through a medium.

Helping Parents Heal
www.helpingparentsheal.org
Providing a wonderful monthly newsletter

Hannah's Heart and Love
www.hannahsheartandlove.org
Providing resources, support, and items to those experiencing the loss of a baby through miscarriage, ectopic pregnancy, stillbirth, and infant death at any gestational age up to one year of age.

Through The Heart
www.throughtheheart.org
Pregnancy loss support and education
Providing free comfort kits on request

FACEBOOK SITES

Forever Our Babies
Here to support all who have been affected by pregnancy, infant or child loss, regardless of gestation or age.

Angel Wings Baby & Child Loss Support
Angel Wings is an awareness & fundraising group for a variety of baby and child loss, miscarriage, stillborn, cot death, ectopic, prem an illness or an accident.

THE GRIEVING PARENT'S HANDBOOK

FACEBOOK SITES
continued

Parents United in Loss
Celebrating our children in spirit

Healing Hearts Baby Loss Comfort
Comfort and support for the bereaved

Grieving Mothers
Comfort and Support for bereaved mothers

RECOMMENDED BOOKS

All of these books can be found on www.amazon.com by entering the title and author's name.

Empty Arms
Hope and Support for Those Who Have Suffered a Miscarriage, Stillbirth, or Tubal Pregnancy

by Pam Vredevelt

Empty Cradle, Broken Heart
Surviving the Death of Your Baby

by Deborah L. Davis

Surviving the Loss of a Child
Support for Grieving Parents

by Elizabeth Brown

How to Survive the Loss of a Child
Filling the Emptiness & Rebuilding Your Life

by Catherine Sanders

Growing Up in Heaven
The Eternal Connection Between Parent and Child

by James Van Praagh

Soul Smart
What the Dead Teach About Spirit Communication

by Susanne Wilson

A Broken Heart Still Beats After Your Child Dies
by Anne McCracken & Mary Semel

Lost and Found
A Mother Connects-Up With Her Son In Spirit

by Sheri Perl

Stephen Lives
My son Steven: His Life, Suicide and Afterlife

by Anne Puryear

My Son and The Afterlife
Conversations from the Other Side

by Elisa Medhus MD

16 Minutes
When One Breath Ends, Another Begins

by Roland Comtois

Soul Shift
Finding Where the Dead Go

by Mark Ireland

Your Soul's Plan
Discovering the Real Meaning of the Life You Planned Before You Were Born

by Robert Schwartz

THE PRAYER TEAM

The Prayer Team consists of
bereaved parents from all over the world.

These parents join together in prayer for the deceased children
who have been registered with The Prayer Registry.

The Prayer Registry is a free service for all bereaved parents.
It ensures that your child will not be forgotten
as each year, going forward,
your child will receive mass prayer
on the anniversary day of his or her passing.

To register your child
and become a member of The Prayer Team
send his or her full name and their passing date
to Sheri at:

theprayerregistry@gmail.com

You are all welcome.

www.ingramcontent.com/pod-product-compliance
Lightning Source LLC
Chambersburg PA
CBHW060521300426
44112CB00017B/2748